The Waggoner & Other Works
by William Wordsworth

William Wordsworth was born on 7 April, 1770 in Cockermouth, in Cumbria, northwest England.

Wordsworth spent his early years in his beloved Lake District often with his sister, Dorothy. The English lakes could terrify as well as nurture, and as Wordsworth would write "I grew up fostered alike by beauty and by fear,"

After being schooled at Hawkshead he went to St. John's College, Cambridge but not liking the competitive nature of the place idled his way through saying he "was not for that hour, nor for that place."

Whilst still at Cambridge he travelled to France. He was immediately taken by the Revolutionary fervor and the confluence of a set of great ideals and rallying calls for the people of France.

In his early twenties he ventured again to France and fathered an illegitimate child. He would not see that daughter till she was 9 owing to the tensions and hostilities between England and France.

There now followed a period of three to four years that plagued Wordsworth with doubt. He was now in his early thirties but had no profession, was rootless and virtually penniless.

Although his career was not on track he did manage to publish two volumes, both in 1793; An Evening Walk and Descriptive Sketches.

This dark period ended in 1795. A legacy of £900 received from Raisley Calvert enabled Wordsworth to pursue a literary career in earnest.

In 1797 he became great friends with a fellow poet, Samuel Taylor Coleridge. They formed a partnership that would change both their lives and the course of English poetry.

Their aim was for a decisive break with the strictures of Neoclassical verse. In 1798 the ground breaking Lyrical Ballads was published. Wordsworth wrote in the preface "the spontaneous overflow of powerful feelings: it takes its origin from emotion recollected in tranquility." Most of the poems were dramatic in form, designed to reveal the character of the speaker. Thus the poems set forth a new style, a new vocabulary, and new subjects for poetry.

Coleridge had also conceived of an enormous poem to be called "The Brook," in which he proposed to treat all science, philosophy, and religion, but soon laid the burden of writing it to Wordsworth. To test his powers for that endeavour, Wordsworth began writing the autobiographical poem that would absorb him for the next 40 years, and which was eventually published as The Prelude, or, Growth of a Poet's Mind.

By the 1820s, the critical acclaim for Wordsworth was growing, but perhaps his best years of work were behind him. Nonetheless he continued to write and to revise previous works.

With the death is 1843 of his friend and Poet Laureate Robert Southey, Wordsworth was offered the position. He accepted despite saying he wouldn't write any poetry as Poet Laureate. And indeed he didn't.

Wordsworth died of pleurisy on 23 April 1850. He was buried in St Oswald's church Grasmere.

Index of Contents
THE WAGGONER
CANTO FIRST
CASNTO SECOND
CANTO THIRD
CANTO FOURTH
LAODAMIA
TO THE REV. DR. WORDSWORTH
A SERIES OF SONNETS TO THE RIVER DUDDON, 1820.
I
II
III
IV
V
VI. FLOWERS
VII
VIII
IX. THE STEPPING-STONES
X. THE SAME SUBJECT
XI. THE FAERY CHASM
XII. HINTS FOR THE FANCY
XIII. OPEN PROSPECT
XIV
XV
XVI. AMERICAN TRADITION
XVII. RETURN
XVIII. SEATHWAITE CHAPEL
XIX. TRIBUTARY STREAM
XX. THE PLAIN OF DONNERDALE
XXI
XXII. TRADITION
XXIII. SHEEP-WASHING
XXIV. THE RESTING-PLACE
XXV
XXVI
XXVII
XXVIII. JOURNEY RENEWED
XXIX
XXX

XXXI
XXXII
XXXIII. CONCLUSION
XXXIV. AFTER-THOUGHT
WILLIAM WORDSWORTH – A SHORT BIOGRAPHY
WILLIAM WORDSWORTH – A CONCISE BIBLIOGRAPHY

THE WAGGONER

CANTO FIRST

'Tis spent—this burning day of June!
Soft darkness o'er its latest gleams is stealing;
The buzzing dor-hawk, round and round, is wheeling,—
That solitary bird
Is all that can be heard
In silence deeper far than that of deepest noon!
Confiding Glow-worms, 'tis a night
Propitious to your earth-born light!
But, where the scattered stars are seen
In hazy straits the clouds between,
Each, in his station twinkling not,
Seems changed into a pallid spot.
The mountains against heaven's grave weight
Rise up, and grow to wondrous height.
The air, as in a lion's den,
Is close and hot;—and now and then
Comes a tired and sultry breeze
With a haunting and a panting,
Like the stifling of disease;
But the dews allay the heat,
And the silence makes it sweet.
Hush, there is some one on the stir!
'Tis Benjamin the Waggoner;
Who long hath trod this toilsome way,
Companion of the night and day.
That far-off tinkling's drowsy cheer,
Mixed with a faint yet grating sound
In a moment lost and found,
The Wain announces—by whose side
Along the banks of Rydal Mere
He paces on, a trusty Guide,—
Listen! you can scarcely hear!
Hither he his course is bending;—

Now he leaves the lower ground,
And up the craggy hill ascending
Many a stop and stay he makes,
Many a breathing-fit he takes;—
Steep the way and wearisome,
Yet all the while his whip is dumb!
The Horses have worked with right good-will,
And so have gained the top of the hill;
He was patient, they were strong,
And now they smoothly glide along,
Recovering breath, and pleased to win
The praises of mild Benjamin.
Heaven shield him from mishap and snare!
But why so early with this prayer?—
Is it for threatenings in the sky?
Or for some other danger nigh?
No; none is near him yet, though he
Be one of much infirmity;
For at the bottom of the brow,
Where once the DOVE and OLIVE-BOUGH
Offered a greeting of good ale
To all who entered Grasmere Vale;
And called on him who must depart
To leave it with a jovial heart;
There, where the DOVE and OLIVE-BOUGH
Once hung, a Poet harbours now,
A simple water-drinking Bard;
Why need our Hero then (though frail
His best resolves) be on his guard?
He marches by, secure and bold;
Yet while he thinks on times of old,
It seems that all looks wondrous cold;
He shrugs his shoulders, shakes his head,
And, for the honest folk within,
It is a doubt with Benjamin
Whether they be alive or dead!
'Here' is no danger,—none at all!
Beyond his wish he walks secure;
But pass a mile—and 'then' for trial,—-
Then for the pride of self-denial;
If he resist that tempting door,
Which with such friendly voice will call;
If he resist those casement panes,
And that bright gleam which thence will fall
Upon his Leaders' bells and manes,
Inviting him with cheerful lure:
For still, though all be dark elsewhere,
Some shining notice will be 'there',

Of open house and ready fare.
The place to Benjamin right well
Is known, and by as strong a spell
As used to be that sign of love
And hope—the OLIVE-BOUGH and DOVE;
He knows it to his cost, good Man!
Who does not know the famous SWAN?
Object uncouth! and yet our boast,
For it was painted by the Host;
His own conceit the figure planned,
'Twas coloured all by his own hand;
And that frail Child of thirsty clay,
Of whom I sing this rustic lay,
Could tell with self-dissatisfaction
Quaint stories of the bird's attraction!
Well! that is past—and in despite
Of open door and shining light.
And now the conqueror essays
The long ascent of Dunmail-raise;
And with his team is gentle here
As when he clomb from Rydal Mere;
His whip they do not dread—his voice
They only hear it to rejoice.
To stand or go is at 'their' pleasure;
Their efforts and their time they measure
By generous pride within the breast;
And, while they strain, and while they rest,
He thus pursues his thoughts at leisure.
Now am I fairly safe to-night—
And with proud cause my heart is light:
I trespassed lately worse than ever—
But Heaven has blest a good endeavour;
And, to my soul's content, I find
The evil One is left behind.
Yes, let my master fume and fret,
Here am I—with my horses yet!
My jolly team, he finds that ye
Will work for nobody but me!
Full proof of this the Country gained;
It knows how ye were vexed and strained,
And forced unworthy stripes to bear,
When trusted to another's care.
Here was it—on this rugged slope,
Which now ye climb with heart and hope,
I saw you, between rage and fear,
Plunge, and fling back a spiteful ear,
And ever more and more confused,
As ye were more and more abused:

As chance would have it, passing by
I saw you in that jeopardy:
A word from me was like a charm;
Ye pulled together with one mind;
And your huge burthen, safe from harm,
Moved like a vessel in the wind!
—Yes, without me, up hills so high
'Tis vain to strive for mastery.
Then grieve not, jolly team! though tough
The road we travel, steep, and rough;
Though Rydal-heights and Dunmail-raise,
And all their fellow banks and braes,
Full often make you stretch and strain,
And halt for breath and halt again,
Yet to their sturdiness 'tis owing
That side by side we still are going!
While Benjamin in earnest mood
His meditations thus pursued,
A storm, which had been smothered long,
Was growing inwardly more strong;
And, in its struggles to get free,
Was busily employed as he.
The thunder had begun to growl—
He heard not, too intent of soul;
The air was now without a breath—
He marked not that 'twas still as death.
But soon large rain-drops on his head
Fell with the weight of drops of lead;—
He starts—and takes, at the admonition,
A sage survey of his condition.
The road is black before his eyes,
Glimmering faintly where it lies;
Black is the sky—and every hill,
Up to the sky, is blacker still—
Sky, hill, and dale, one dismal room,
Hung round and overhung with gloom;
Save that above a single height
Is to be seen a lurid light,
Above Helm-crag—a streak half dead,
A burning of portentous red;
And near that lurid light, full well
The ASTROLOGER, sage Sidrophel,
Where at his desk and book he sits,
Puzzling aloft his curious wits;
He whose domain is held in common
With no one but the ANCIENT WOMAN,
Cowering beside her rifted cell,
As if intent on magic spell;—

Dread pair, that, spite of wind and weather,
Still sit upon Helm-crag together!
The ASTROLOGER was not unseen
By solitary Benjamin;
But total darkness came anon,
And he and everything was gone:
And suddenly a ruffling breeze,
(That would have rocked the sounding trees
Had aught of sylvan growth been there)
Swept through the Hollow long and bare:
The rain rushed down—the road was battered,
As with the force of billows shattered;
The horses are dismayed, nor know
Whether they should stand or go;
And Benjamin is groping near them
Sees nothing, and can scarcely hear them.
He is astounded,—wonder not,—
With such a charge in such a spot;
Astounded in the mountain gap
With thunder-peals, clap after clap,
Close-treading on the silent flashes—
And somewhere, as he thinks, by crashes
Among the rocks; with weight of rain,
And sullen motions long and slow,
That to a dreary distance go—
Till, breaking in upon the dying strain,
A rending o'er his head begins the fray again.
Meanwhile, uncertain what to do,
And oftentimes compelled to halt,
The horses cautiously pursue
Their way, without mishap or fault;
And now have reached that pile of stones,
Heaped over brave King Dunmail's bones;
His who had once supreme command,
Last king of rocky Cumberland;
His bones, and those of all his Power
Slain here in a disastrous hour!
When, passing through this narrow strait,
Stony, and dark, and desolate,
Benjamin can faintly hear
A voice that comes from some one near,
A female voice—Whoe'er you be,
Stop," it exclaimed, "and pity me!"
And, less in pity than in wonder,
Amid the darkness and the thunder,
The Waggoner, with prompt command,
Summons his horses to a stand.
While, with increasing agitation,

The Woman urged her supplication,
In rueful words, with sobs between—
The voice of tears that fell unseen;
There came a flash—a startling glare,
And all Seat-Sandal was laid bare!
'Tis not a time for nice suggestion,
And Benjamin, without a question,
Taking her for some way-worn rover,
Said, "Mount, and get you under cover!"
Another voice, in tone as hoarse
As a swoln brook with rugged course,
Cried out, "Good brother, why so fast?
I've had a glimpse of you—'avast!'
Or, since it suits you to be civil,
Take her at once—for good and evil!"
"It is my Husband," softly said
The Woman, as if half afraid:
By this time she was snug within,
Through help of honest Benjamin;
She and her Babe, which to her breast
With thankfulness the Mother pressed;
And now the same strong voice more near
Said cordially, "My Friend, what cheer?
Rough doings these! as God's my judge,
The sky owes somebody a grudge!
We've had in half an hour or less
A twelvemonth's terror and distress!"
Then Benjamin entreats the Man
Would mount, too, quickly as he can:
The Sailor—Sailor now no more,
But such he had been heretofore—
To courteous Benjamin replied,
"Go you your way, and mind not me;
For I must have, whate'er betide,
My Ass and fifty things beside,—
Go, and I'll follow speedily!"
The Waggon moves—and with its load
Descends along the sloping road;
And the rough Sailor instantly
Turns to a little tent hard by:
For when, at closing-in of day,
The family had come that way,
Green pasture and the soft warm air
Tempted them to settle there.—
Green is the grass for beast to graze,
Around the stones of Dunmail-raise!
The Sailor gathers up his bed,
Takes down the canvas overhead;

And, after farewell to the place,
A parting word—though not of grace,
Pursues, with Ass and all his store,
The way the Waggon went before.

CANTO SECOND

IF Wytheburn's modest House of prayer,
As lowly as the lowliest dwelling,
Had, with its belfry's humble stock,
A little pair that hang in air,
Been mistress also of a clock,
(And one, too, not in crazy plight)
Twelve strokes that clock would have been telling
Under the brow of old Helvellyn—
Its bead-roll of midnight,
Then, when the Hero of my tale
Was passing by, and, down the vale
(The vale now silent, hushed I ween
As if a storm had never been)
Proceeding with a mind at ease;
While the old Familiar of the seas,
Intent to use his utmost haste,
Gained ground upon the Waggon fast,
And gives another lusty cheer;
For spite of rumbling of the wheels,
A welcome greeting he can hear;—
It is a fiddle in its glee
Dinning from the CHERRY TREE!
Thence the sound—the light is there—
As Benjamin is now aware,
Who, to his inward thoughts confined,
Had almost reached the festive door,
When, startled by the Sailor's roar,
He hears a sound and sees a light,
And in a moment calls to mind
That 'tis the village MERRY-NIGHT!
Although before in no dejection,
At this insidious recollection
His heart with sudden joy is filled,—
His ears are by the music thrilled,
His eyes take pleasure in the road
Glittering before him bright and broad;
And Benjamin is wet and cold,
And there are reasons manifold
That make the good, tow'rds which he's yearning,

Look fairly like a lawful earning.
Nor has thought time to come and go,
To vibrate between yes and no;
For, cries the Sailor, "Glorious chance
That blew us hither!—let him dance,
Who can or will!—my honest soul,
Our treat shall be a friendly bowl!"
He draws him to the door—"Come in,
Come, come," cries he to Benjamin!
And Benjamin—ah, woe is me!
Gave the word—the horses heard
And halted, though reluctantly.
"Blithe souls and lightsome hearts have we,
Feasting at the CHERRY TREE!"
This was the outside proclamation,
This was the inside salutation;
What bustling—jostling—high and low!
A universal overflow!
What tankards foaming from the tap!
What store of cakes in every lap!
What thumping—stumping—overhead!
The thunder had not been more busy:
With such a stir you would have said,
This little place may well be dizzy!
'Tis who can dance with greatest vigour—
'Tis what can be most prompt and eager;
As if it heard the fiddle's call,
The pewter clatters on the wall;
The very bacon shows its feeling,
Swinging from the smoky ceiling!
A steaming bowl, a blazing fire,
What greater good can heart desire?
'Twere worth a wise man's while to try
The utmost anger of the sky:
To 'seek' for thoughts of a gloomy cast,
If such the bright amends at last.
Now should you say I judge amiss,
The CHERRY TREE shows proof of this;
For soon of all the happy there,
Our Travellers are the happiest pair;
All care with Benjamin is gone—
A Caesar past the Rubicon!
He thinks not of his long, long strife;—
The Sailor, Man by nature gay,
Hath no resolves to throw away;
And he hath now forgot his Wife,
Hath quite forgotten her—or may be
Thinks her the luckiest soul on earth,

Within that warm and peaceful berth,
Under cover,
Terror over,
Sleeping by her sleeping Baby,
With bowl that sped from hand to hand,
The gladdest of the gladsome band,
Amid their own delight and fun,
They hear—when every dance is done,
When every whirling bout is o'er—
The fiddle's 'squeak'—that call to bliss,
Ever followed by a kiss;
They envy not the happy lot,
But enjoy their own the more!
While thus our jocund Travellers fare,
Up springs the Sailor from his chair—
Limps (for I might have told before
That he was lame) across the floor—
Is gone—returns—and with a prize;
With what?—a Ship of lusty size;
A gallant stately Man-of-war,
Fixed on a smoothly-sliding car.
Surprise to all, but most surprise
To Benjamin, who rubs his eyes,
Not knowing that he had befriended
A Man so gloriously attended!
"This," cries the Sailor, "a Third-rate is—
Stand back, and you shall see her gratis!
This was the Flag-ship at the Nile,
The Vanguard—you may smirk and smile,
But, pretty Maid, if you look near,
You'll find you've much in little here!
A nobler ship did never swim,
And you shall see her in full trim:
I'll set, my friends, to do you honour,
Set every inch of sail upon her."
So said, so done; and masts, sails, yards,
He names them all; and interlards
His speech with uncouth terms of art,
Accomplished in the showman's part;
And then, as from a sudden check,
Cries out—"'Tis there, the quarter-deck
On which brave Admiral Nelson stood—
A sight that would have roused your blood!
One eye he had, which, bright as ten,
Burned like a fire among his men;
Let this be land, and that be sea,
Here lay the French—and 'thus' came we!"
Hushed was by this the fiddle's sound,

The dancers all were gathered round,
And, such the stillness of the house,
You might have heard a nibbling mouse;
While, borrowing helps where'er he may,
The Sailor through the story runs
Of ships to ships and guns to guns;
And does his utmost to display
The dismal conflict, and the might
And terror of that marvellous night!
"A bowl, a bowl of double measure,"
Cries Benjamin, "a draught of length,
To Nelson, England's pride and treasure,
Her bulwark and her tower of strength!"
When Benjamin had seized the bowl,
The mastiff, from beneath the waggon,
Where he lay, watchful as a dragon,
Rattled his chain;—'twas all in vain,
For Benjamin, triumphant soul!
He heard the monitory growl;
Heard—and in opposition quaffed
A deep, determined, desperate draught!
Nor did the battered Tar forget,
Or flinch from what he deemed his debt:
Then, like a hero crowned with laurel,
Back to her place the ship he led;
Wheeled her back in full apparel;
And so, flag flying at mast head,
Re-yoked her to the Ass:—anon,
Cries Benjamin, "We must be gone.
Thus, after two hours' hearty stay,
Again behold them on their way!

CANTO THIRD

Right gladly had the horses stirred,
When they the wished-for greeting heard,
The whip's loud notice from the door,
That they were free to move once more.
You think, those doings must have bred
In them disheartening doubts and dread;
No, not a horse of all the eight,
Although it be a moonless night,
Fears either for himself or freight;
For this they know (and let it hide,
In part, the offences of their guide)
That Benjamin, with clouded brains,

Is worth the best with all their pains;
And, if they had a prayer to make,
The prayer would be that they may take
With him whatever comes in course,
The better fortune or the worse;
That no one else may have business near them,
And, drunk or sober, he may steer them.
So, forth in dauntless mood they fare,
And with them goes the guardian pair.
Now, heroes, for the true commotion,
The triumph of your late devotion
Can aught on earth impede delight,
Still mounting to a higher height;
And higher still—a greedy flight!
Can any low-born care pursue her,
Can any mortal clog come to her?
No notion have they—not a thought,
That is from joyless regions brought!
And, while they coast the silent lake,
Their inspiration I partake;
Share their empyreal spirits—yea,
With their enraptured vision, see—
O fancy—what a jubilee!
What shifting pictures—clad in gleams
Of colour bright as feverish dreams!
Earth, spangled sky, and lake serene,
Involved and restless all—a scene
Pregnant with mutual exaltation,
Rich change, and multiplied creation!
This sight to me the Muse imparts;—
And then, what kindness in their hearts!
What tears of rapture, what vow-making,
Profound entreaties, and hand-shaking!
What solemn, vacant, interlacing,
As if they'd fall asleep embracing!
Then, in the turbulence of glee,
And in the excess of amity,
Says Benjamin, "That Ass of thine,
He spoils thy sport, and hinders mine:
If he were tethered to the waggon,
He'd drag as well what he is dragging,
And we, as brother should with brother,
Might trudge it alongside each other!"
Forthwith, obedient to command,
The horses made a quiet stand;
And to the waggon's skirts was tied
The Creature, by the Mastiff's side,
The Mastiff wondering, and perplext

With dread of what will happen next;
And thinking it but sorry cheer,
To have such company so near!
This new arrangement made, the Wain
Through the still night proceeds again;
No Moon hath risen her light to lend;
But indistinctly may be kenned
The VANGUARD, following close behind,
Sails spread, as if to catch the wind!
"Thy wife and child are snug and warm,
Thy ship will travel without harm;
I like," said Benjamin, "her shape and stature:
And this of mine—this bulky creature
Of which I have the steering—this,
Seen fairly, is not much amiss!
We want your streamers, friend, you know;
But, altogether as we go,
We make a kind of handsome show!
Among these hills, from first to last,
We've weathered many a furious blast;
Hard passage forcing on, with head
Against the storm, and canvas spread.
I hate a boaster; but to thee
Will say't, who know'st both land and sea,
The unluckiest hulk that stems the brine
Is hardly worse beset than mine,
When cross-winds on her quarter beat;
And, fairly lifted from my feet,
I stagger onward—heaven knows how;
But not so pleasantly as now:
Poor pilot I, by snows confounded,
And many a foundrous pit surrounded!
Yet here we are, by night and day
Grinding through rough and smooth our way;
Through foul and fair our task fulfilling;
And long shall be so yet—God willing!"
"Ay," said the Tar, "through fair and foul—
But save us from yon screeching owl!"
That instant was begun a fray
Which called their thoughts another way:
The mastiff, ill-conditioned carl!
What must he do but growl and snarl,
Still more and more dissatisfied
With the meek comrade at his side!
Till, not incensed though put to proof,
The Ass, uplifting a hind hoof,
Salutes the Mastiff on the head;
And so were better manners bred,

And all was calmed and quieted.
"Yon screech-owl," says the Sailor, turning
Back to his former cause of mourning,
"Yon owl!—pray God that all be well!
'Tis worse than any funeral bell;
As sure as I've the gift of sight,
We shall be meeting ghosts to-night!"
—Said Benjamin, "This whip shall lay
A thousand, if they cross our way.
I know that Wanton's noisy station,
I know him and his occupation;
The jolly bird hath learned his cheer
Upon the banks of Windermere;
Where a tribe of them make merry,
Mocking the Man that keeps the ferry;
Hallooing from an open throat,
Like travellers shouting for a boat.
—The tricks he learned at Windermere
This vagrant owl is playing here—
That is the worst of his employment:
He's at the top of his enjoyment!"
This explanation stilled the alarm,
Cured the foreboder like a charm;
This, and the manner, and the voice,
Summoned the Sailor to rejoice;
His heart is up—he fears no evil
From life or death, from man or devil;
He wheels—and, making many stops,
Brandished his crutch against the mountain tops;
And, while he talked of blows and scars,
Benjamin, among the stars,
Beheld a dancing—and a glancing;
Such retreating and advancing
As, I ween, was never seen
In bloodiest battle since the days of Mars!

CANTO FOURTH

Thus they, with freaks of proud delight,
Beguile the remnant of the night;
And many a snatch of jovial song
Regales them as they wind along;
While to the music, from on high,
The echoes make a glad reply.—
But the sage Muse the revel heeds
No farther than her story needs;

Nor will she servilely attend
The loitering journey to its end.
—Blithe spirits of her own impel
The Muse, who scents the morning air,
To take of this transported pair
A brief and unreproved farewell;
To quit the slow-paced waggon's side,
And wander down yon hawthorn dell,
With murmuring Greta for her guide.
—There doth she ken the awful form
Of Raven-crag—black as a storm—
Glimmering through the twilight pale;
And Ghimmer-crag, his tall twin brother,
Each peering forth to meet the other:—
And, while she roves through St. John's Vale,
Along the smooth unpathwayed plain,
By sheep-track or through cottage lane,
Where no disturbance comes to intrude
Upon the pensive solitude,
Her unsuspecting eye, perchance,
With the rude shepherd's favoured glance,
Beholds the faeries in array,
Whose party-coloured garments gay
The silent company betray:
Red, green, and blue; a moment's sight!
For Skiddaw-top with rosy light
Is touched—and all the band take flight.
—Fly also, Muse! and from the dell
Mount to the ridge of Nathdale Fell;
Thence, look thou forth o'er wood and lawn
Hoar with the frost-like dews of dawn;
Across yon meadowy bottom look,
Where close fogs hide their parent brook;
And see, beyond that hamlet small,
The ruined towers of Threlkeld-hall,
Lurking in a double shade,
By trees and lingering twilight made!
There, at Blencathara's rugged feet,
Sir Lancelot gave a safe retreat
To noble Clifford; from annoy
Concealed the persecuted boy,
Well pleased in rustic garb to feed
His flock, and pipe on shepherd's reed
Among this multitude of hills,
Crags, woodlands, waterfalls, and rills;
Which soon the morning shall enfold,
From east to west, in ample vest
Of massy gloom and radiance bold.

The mists, that o'er the streamlet's bed
Hung low, begin to rise and spread;
Even while I speak, their skirts of grey
Are smitten by a silver ray;
And lo!—up Castrigg's naked steep
(Where, smoothly urged, the vapours sweep
Along—and scatter and divide,
Like fleecy clouds self-multiplied)
The stately waggon is ascending,
With faithful Benjamin attending,
Apparent now beside his team—
Now lost amid a glittering steam:
And with him goes his Sailor-friend,
By this time near their journey's end;
And, after their high-minded riot,
Sickening into thoughtful quiet;
As if the morning's pleasant hour
Had for their joys a killing power.
And, sooth, for Benjamin a vein
Is opened of still deeper pain
As if his heart by notes were stung
From out the lowly hedge-rows flung;
As if the Warbler lost in light
Reproved his soarings of the night,
In strains of rapture pure and holy
Upbraided his distempered folly.
Drooping is he, his step is dull;
But the horses stretch and pull;
With increasing vigour climb,
Eager to repair lost time;
Whether, by their own desert,
Knowing what cause there is for shame,
They are labouring to avert
As much as may be of the blame,
Which, they foresee, must soon alight
Upon 'his' head, whom, in despite
Of all his failings, they love best;
Whether for him they are distrest,
Or, by length of fasting roused,
Are impatient to be housed:
Up against the hill they strain
Tugging at the iron chain,
Tugging all with might and main,
Last and foremost, every horse
To the utmost of his force!
And the smoke and respiration,
Rising like an exhalation,
Blend with the mist—a moving shroud

To form, an undissolving cloud;
Which, with slant ray, the merry sun
Takes delight to play upon.
Never golden-haired Apollo,
Pleased some favourite chief to follow
Through accidents of peace or war,
In a perilous moment threw
Around the object of his care
Veil of such celestial hue;
Interposed so bright a screen—
Him and his enemies between!
Alas! what boots it?—who can hide,
When the malicious Fates are bent
On working out an ill intent?
Can destiny be turned aside?
No—sad progress of my story!
Benjamin, this outward glory
Cannot shield thee from thy Master,
Who from Keswick has pricked forth,
Sour and surly as the north;
And, in fear of some disaster,
Comes to give what help he may,
And to hear what thou canst say;
If, as needs he must forebode,
Thou hast been loitering on the road!
His fears, his doubts, may now take flight—
The wished-for object is in sight;
Yet, trust the Muse, it rather hath
Stirred him up to livelier wrath;
Which he stifles, moody man!
With all the patience that he can;
To the end that, at your meeting,
He may give thee decent greeting.
There he is—resolved to stop,
Till the waggon gains the top;
But stop he cannot—must advance:
Him Benjamin, with lucky glance,
Espies—and instantly is ready,
Self-collected, poised, and steady:
And, to be the better seen,
Issues from his radiant shroud,
From his close-attending cloud,
With careless air and open mien.
Erect his port, and firm his going;
So struts yon cock that now is crowing;
And the morning light in grace
Strikes upon his lifted face,
Hurrying the pallid hue away

That might his trespasses betray.
But what can all avail to clear him,
Or what need of explanation,
Parley or interrogation?
For the Master sees, alas!
That unhappy Figure near him,
Limping o'er the dewy grass,
Where the road it fringes, sweet,
Soft and cool to way-worn feet;
And, O indignity! an Ass,
By his noble Mastiff's side,
Tethered to the waggon's tail:
And the ship, in all her pride,
Following after in full sail!
Not to speak of babe and mother;
Who, contented with each other,
And snug as birds in leafy arbour,
Find, within, a blessed harbour!
With eager eyes the Master pries;
Looks in and out, and through and through;
Says nothing—till at last he spies
A wound upon the Mastiff's head,
A wound, where plainly might be read
What feats an Ass's hoof can do!
But drop the rest:—this aggravation,
This complicated provocation,
A hoard of grievances unsealed;
All past forgiveness it repealed;
And thus, and through distempered blood
On both sides, Benjamin the good,
The patient, and the tender-hearted,
Was from his team and waggon parted;
When duty of that day was o'er,
Laid down his whip—and served no more,—
Nor could the waggon long survive,
Which Benjamin had ceased to drive:
It lingered on;—guide after guide
Ambitiously the office tried;
But each unmanageable hill
Called for 'his' patience and 'his' skill;—
And sure it is, that through this night,
And what the morning brought to light,
Two losses had we to sustain,
We lost both WAGGONER and WAIN!

———————

Accept, O Friend, for praise or blame,

The gift of this adventurous song;
A record which I dared to frame,
Though timid scruples checked me long;
They checked me—and I left the theme
Untouched—in spite of many a gleam
Of fancy which thereon was shed,
Like pleasant sunbeams shifting still
Upon the side of a distant hill:
But Nature might not be gainsaid;
For what I have and what I miss
I sing of these;—it makes my bliss!
Nor is it I who play the part,
But a shy spirit in my heart,
That comes and goes—will sometimes leap
From hiding-places ten years deep;
Or haunts me with familiar face,
Returning, like a ghost unlaid,
Until the debt I owe be paid.
Forgive me, then; for I had been
On friendly terms with this Machine:
In him, while he was wont to trace
Our roads, through many a long year's space,
A living almanack had we;
We had a speaking diary,
That in this uneventful place
Gave to the days a mark and name
By which we knew them when they came.
—Yes, I, and all about me here,
Through all the changes of the year,
Had seen him through the mountains go,
In pomp of mist or pomp of snow,
Majestically huge and slow:
Or, with a milder grace adorning
The landscape of a summer's morning;
While Grasmere smoothed her liquid plain
The moving image to detain;
And mighty Fairfield, with a chime
Of echoes, to his march kept time;
When little other business stirred,
And little other sound was heard;
In that delicious hour of balm,
Stillness, solitude, and calm,
While yet the valley is arrayed,
On this side with a sober shade;
On that is prodigally bright—
Crag, lawn, and wood—with rosy light.
—But most of all, thou Lordly Wain!
I wish to have thee here again,

When windows flap and chimney roars,
And all is dismal out of doors;
And, sitting by my fire, I see
Eight sorry carts, no less a train;
Unworthy successors of thee,
Come straggling through the wind and rain!
And oft, as they pass slowly on,
Beneath my windows, one by one,
See, perched upon the naked height
The summit of a cumbrous freight,
A single traveller—and there
Another; then perhaps a pair—
The lame, the sickly, and the old;
Men, women, heartless with the cold;
And babes in wet and starveling plight
Which once, be weather as it might,
Had still a nest within a nest,
Thy shelter—and their mother's breast!
Then most of all, then far the most,
Do I regret what we have lost;
Am grieved for that unhappy sin
Which robbed us of good Benjamin;
And of his stately Charge, which none
Could keep alive when He was gone!

1805.

LAODAMIA

"With sacrifice before the rising morn
Vows have I made by fruitless hope inspired;
And from the infernal Gods, 'mid shades forlorn
Of night, my slaughtered Lord have I required:
Celestial pity I again implore;—
Restore him to my sight—great Jove, restore!"

So speaking, and by fervent love endowed
With faith, the Suppliant heavenward lifts her hands;
While, like the sun emerging from a cloud,
Her countenance brightens—and her eye expands;
Her bosom heaves and spreads, her stature grows;
And she expects the issue in repose.

O terror! what hath she perceived?—O joy!
What doth she look on?—whom doth she behold?
Her Hero slain upon the beach of Troy?
His vital presence? his corporeal mould?
It is—if sense deceive her not—'tis He!
And a God leads him, winged Mercury!

Mild Hermes spake—and touched her with his wand
That calms all fear; "Such grace hath crowned thy prayer,
Laodamia! that at Jove's command
Thy Husband walks the paths of upper air:
He comes to tarry with thee three hours' space;
Accept the gift, behold him face to face!"

Forth sprang the impassioned Queen her Lord to clasp;
Again that consummation she essayed;
But unsubstantial Form eludes her grasp
As often as that eager grasp was made.
The Phantom parts—but parts to re-unite,
And re-assume his place before her sight.

"Protesilaus, lo! thy guide is gone!
Confirm, I pray, the vision with thy voice:
This is our palace,—yonder is thy throne;
Speak, and the floor thou tread'st on will rejoice.
Not to appal me have the gods bestowed
This precious boon; and blest a sad abode."

"Great Jove, Laodamia! doth not leave
His gifts imperfect:—Spectre though I be,
I am not sent to scare thee or deceive;
But in reward of thy fidelity.
And something also did my worth obtain;
For fearless virtue bringeth boundless gain.

"Thou knowest, the Delphic oracle foretold
That the first Greek who touched the Trojan strand
Should die; but me the threat could not withhold:
A generous cause a victim did demand;
And forth I leapt upon the sandy plain;
A self-devoted chief—by Hector slain."

"Supreme of Heroes—bravest, noblest, best!
Thy matchless courage I bewail no more,
Which then, when tens of thousands were deprest
By doubt, propelled thee to the fatal shore;
Thou found'st—and I forgive thee—here thou art—
A nobler counsellor than my poor heart.

"But thou, though capable of sternest deed,
Wert kind as resolute, and good as brave;
And he, whose power restores thee, hath decreed
Thou should'st elude the malice of the grave:
Redundant are thy locks, thy lips as fair
As when their breath enriched Thessalian air.

"No Spectre greets me,—no vain Shadow this;
Come, blooming Hero, place thee by my side!
Give, on this well-known couch, one nuptial kiss
To me, this day, a second time thy bride!"
Jove frowned in heaven: the conscious Parcae threw
Upon those roseate lips a Stygian hue.

"This visage tells thee that my doom is past:
Nor should the change be mourned, even if the joys
Of sense were able to return as fast
And surely as they vanish. Earth destroys
Those raptures duly—Erebus disdains:
Calm pleasures there abide—majestic pains.

"Be taught, O faithful Consort, to control
Rebellious passion: for the Gods approve
The depth, and not the tumult, of the soul;
A fervent, not ungovernable, love.
Thy transports moderate; and meekly mourn
When I depart, for brief is my sojourn—"

"Ah, wherefore?—Did not Hercules by force
Wrest from the guardian Monster of the tomb
Alcestis, a reanimated corse,
Given back to dwell on earth in vernal bloom?
Medea's spells dispersed the weight of years,
And Aeson stood a youth 'mid youthful peers.

"The Gods to us are merciful—and they
Yet further may relent: for mightier far
Than strength of nerve and sinew, or the sway
Of magic potent over sun and star,
Is love, though oft to agony distrest,
And though his favourite seat be feeble woman's breast.

"But if thou goest, I follow—" "Peace!" he said,—
She looked upon him and was calmed and cheered;
The ghastly colour from his lips had fled;
In his deportment, shape, and mien, appeared
Elysian beauty, melancholy grace,

Brought from a pensive though a happy place.

He spake of love, such love as Spirits feel
In worlds whose course is equable and pure;
No fears to beat away—no strife to heal—
The past unsighed for, and the future sure;
Spake of heroic arts in graver mood
Revived, with finer harmony pursued;

Of all that is most beauteous—imaged there
In happier beauty; more pellucid streams,
An ampler ether, a diviner air,
And fields invested with purpureal gleams;
Climes which the sun, who sheds the brightest day
Earth knows, is all unworthy to survey.

Yet there the Soul shall enter which hath earned
That privilege by virtue.—"Ill," said he,
"The end of man's existence I discerned,
Who from ignoble games and revelry
Could draw, when we had parted, vain delight,
While tears were thy best pastime, day and night;

"And while my youthful peers before my eyes
(Each hero following his peculiar bent)
Prepared themselves for glorious enterprise
By martial sports,—or, seated in the tent,
Chieftains and kings in council were detained;
What time the fleet at Aulis lay enchained.

"The wished-for wind was given:—I then revolved
The oracle, upon the silent sea;
And, if no worthier led the way, resolved
That, of a thousand vessels, mine should be
The foremost prow in pressing to the strand,—
Mine the first blood that tinged the Trojan sand.

"Yet bitter, oft-times bitter, was the pang
When of thy loss I thought, beloved Wife!
On thee too fondly did my memory hang,
And on the joys we shared in mortal life,—
The paths which we had trod—these fountains, flowers
My new-planned cities, and unfinished towers.

"But should suspense permit the Foe to cry,
'Behold they tremble!—haughty their array,
Yet of their number no one dares to die?'
In soul I swept the indignity away:

Old frailties then recurred:—but lofty thought,
In act embodied, my deliverance wrought.

"And Thou, though strong in love, art all too weak
In reason, in self-government too slow;
I counsel thee by fortitude to seek
Our blest re-union in the shades below.
The invisible world with thee hath sympathised;
Be thy affections raised and solemnised.

"Learn, by a mortal yearning, to ascend—
Seeking a higher object. Love was given,
Encouraged, sanctioned, chiefly for that end;
For this the passion to excess was driven—
That self might be annulled: her bondage prove
The fetters of a dream, opposed to love."—

Aloud she shrieked! for Hermes reappears!
Round the dear Shade she would have clung—'tis vain:
The hours are past—too brief had they been years;
And him no mortal effort can detain:
Swift, toward the realms that know not earthly day,
He through the portal takes his silent way,
And on the palace-floor a lifeless corpse She lay.

Thus, all in vain exhorted and reproved,
She perished; and, as for a wilful crime,
By the just Gods whom no weak pity moved,
Was doomed to wear out her appointed time,
Apart from happy Ghosts, that gather flowers
Of blissful quiet 'mid unfading bowers.

—Yet tears to human suffering are due;
And mortal hopes defeated and o'erthrown
Are mourned by man, and not by man alone,
As fondly he believes.—Upon the side
Of Hellespont (such faith was entertained)
A knot of spiry trees for ages grew
From out the tomb of him for whom she died;
And ever, when such stature they had gained
That Ilium's walls were subject to their view,
The trees' tall summits withered at the sight;
A constant interchange of growth and blight!

1814.

TO THE REV. DR. WORDSWORTH

(WITH THE SONNETS TO THE RIVER DUDDON, AND OTHER POEMS IN THIS COLLECTION, 1820)

THE Minstrels played their Christmas tune
To-night beneath my cottage-eaves;
While, smitten by a lofty moon,
The encircling laurels, thick with leaves,
Gave back a rich and dazzling sheen,
That overpowered their natural green.

Through hill and valley every breeze
Had sunk to rest with folded wings:
Keen was the air, but could not freeze,
Nor check, the music of the strings;
So stout and hardy were the band
That scraped the chords with strenuous hand;

And who but listened?--till was paid
Respect to every Inmate's claim:
The greeting given, the music played,
In honour of each household name,
Duly pronounced with lusty call,
And "merry Christmas" wished to all!

O Brother! I revere the choice
That took thee from thy native hills;
And it is given thee to rejoice:
Though public care full often tills
(Heaven only witness of the toil)
A barren and ungrateful soil.

Yet, would that Thou, with me and mine,
Hadst heard this never-failing rite;
And seen on other faces shine
A true revival of the light
Which Nature and these rustic Powers,
In simple childhood, spread through ours.

For pleasure hath not ceased to wait
On these expected annual rounds;
Whether the rich man's sumptuous gate
Call forth the unelaborate sounds,
Or they are offered at the door
That guards the lowliest of the poor.

How touching, when, at midnight, sweep

Snow-muffled winds, and all is dark,
To hear--and sink again to sleep!
Or, at an earlier call, to mark,
By blazing fire, the still suspense
Of self-complacent innocence;

The mutual nod,--the grave disguise
Of hearts with gladness brimming o'er;
And some unbidden tears that rise
For names once heard, and heard no more;
Tears brightened by the serenade
For infant in the cradle laid.

Ah! not for emerald fields alone,
With ambient streams more pure and bright
Than fabled Cytherea's zone
Glittering before the Thunderer's sight,
Is to my heart of hearts endeared
The ground where we were born and reared!

Hail, ancient Manners! sure defence,
Where they survive, of wholesome laws;
Remnants of love whose modest sense
Thus into narrow room withdraws;
Hail, Usages of pristine mould,
And ye that guard them, Mountains old!

Bear with me, Brother! quench the thought
That slights this passion, or condemns;
If thee fond Fancy ever brought
From the proud margin of the Thames,
And Lambeth's venerable towers,
To humbler streams, and greener bowers.

Yes, they can make, who fail to find,
Short leisure even in busiest days;
Moments, to cast a look behind,
And profit by those kindly rays
That through the clouds do sometimes steal,
And all the far-off past reveal.

Hence, while the imperial City's din
Beats frequent on thy satiate ear,
A pleased attention I may win
To agitations less severe,
That neither overwhelm nor cloy,
But fill the hollow vale with joy!

A SERIES OF SONNETS, 1820.

I

Not envying Latian shades--if yet they throw
A grateful coolness round that crystal Spring,
Blandusia, prattling as when long ago
The Sabine Bard was moved her praise to sing;
Careless of flowers that in perennial blow
Round the moist marge of Persian fountains cling;
Heedless of Alpine torrents thundering
Through ice-built arches radiant as heaven's bow;
I seek the birthplace of a native Stream.--
All hail, ye mountains! hail, thou morning light!
Better to breathe at large on this clear height
Than toil in needless sleep from dream to dream:
Pure flow the verse, pure, vigorous, free, and bright,
For Duddon, long-loved Duddon, is my theme!

II

Child of the clouds! remote from every taint
Of sordid industry thy lot is cast;
Thine are the honours of the lofty waste
Not seldom, when with heat the valleys faint,
Thy handmaid Frost with spangled tissue quaint
Thy cradle decks;--to chant thy birth, thou hast
No meaner Poet than the whistling Blast,
And Desolation is thy Patron-saint!
She guards thee, ruthless Power! who would not spare
Those mighty forests, once the bison's screen,
Where stalked the huge deer to his shaggy lair
Through paths and alleys roofed with darkest green;
Thousands of years before the silent air
Was pierced by whizzing shaft of hunter keen!

III

How shall I paint thee?--Be this naked stone
My seat, while I give way to such intent;
Pleased could my verse, a speaking monument,
Make to the eyes of men thy features known.
But as of all those tripping lambs not one

Outruns his fellows, so hath Nature lent
To thy beginning nought that doth present
Peculiar ground for hope to build upon.
To dignify the spot that gives thee birth,
No sign of hoar Antiquity's esteem
Appears, and none of modern Fortune's care;
Yet thou thyself hast round thee shed a gleam
Of brilliant moss, instinct with freshness rare;
Prompt offering to thy Foster-mother, Earth!

IV

Take, cradled Nursling of the mountain, take
This parting glance, no negligent adieu!
A Protean change seems wrought while I pursue
The curves, a loosely-scattered chain doth make;
Or rather thou appear'st a glistering snake,
Silent, and to the gazer's eye untrue,
Thridding with sinuous lapse the rushes, through
Dwarf willows gliding, and by ferny brake.
Starts from a dizzy steep the undaunted Rill
Robed instantly in garb of snow-white foam;
And laughing dares the Adventurer, who hath clomb
So high, a rival purpose to fulfil;
Else let the dastard backward wend, and roam,
Seeking less bold achievement, where he will!

V

Sole listener, Duddon! to the breeze that played
With thy clear voice, I caught the fitful sound
Wafted o'er sullen moss and craggy mound--
Unfruitful solitudes, that seemed to upbraid
The sun in heaven!--but now, to form a shade
For Thee, green alders have together wound
Their foliage; ashes flung their arms around;
And birch-trees risen in silver colonnade.
And thou hast also tempted here to rise,
'Mid sheltering pines, this Cottage rude and grey;
Whose ruddy children, by the mother's eyes
Carelessly watched, sport through the summer day,
Thy pleased associates:--light as endless May
On infant bosoms lonely Nature lies.

VI. FLOWERS

Ere yet our course was graced with social trees
It lacked not old remains of hawthorn bowers,
Where small birds warbled to their paramours;
And, earlier still, was heard the hum of bees;
I saw them ply their harmless robberies,
And caught the fragrance which the sundry flowers,
Fed by the stream with soft perpetual showers,
Plenteously yielded to the vagrant breeze.
There bloomed the strawberry of the wilderness;
The trembling eyebright showed her sapphire blue,
The thyme her purple, like the blush of Even;
And if the breath of some to no caress
Invited, forth they peeped so fair to view,
All kinds alike seemed favourites of Heaven.

VII

"Change me, some God, into that breathing rose!"
The love-sick Stripling fancifully sighs,
The envied flower beholding, as it lies
On Laura's breast, in exquisite repose;
Or he would pass into her bird, that throws
The darts of song from out its wiry cage;
Enraptured,--could he for himself engage
The thousandth part of what the Nymph bestows;
And what the little careless innocent
Ungraciously receives. Too daring choice!
There are whose calmer mind it would content
To be an unculled floweret of the glen,
Fearless of plough and scythe; or darkling wren
That tunes on Duddon's banks her slender voice.

VIII

What aspect bore the Man who roved or fled,
First of his tribe, to this dark dell--who first
In this pellucid Current slaked his thirst?
What hopes came with him? what designs were spread
Along his path? His unprotected bed
What dreams encompassed? Was the intruder nursed
In hideous usages, and rites accursed,
That thinned the living and disturbed the dead?
No voice replies;--both air and earth are mute;
And Thou, blue Streamlet, murmuring yield'st no more
Than a soft record, that, whatever fruit

Of ignorance thou might'st witness heretofore,
Thy function was to heal and to restore,
To soothe and cleanse, not madden and pollute!

IX. THE STEPPING-STONES

The struggling Rill insensibly is grown
Into a Brook of loud and stately march,
Crossed ever and anon by plank or arch;
And, for like use, lo! what might seem a zone
Chosen for ornament--stone matched with stone
In studied symmetry, with interspace
For the clear waters to pursue their race
Without restraint. How swiftly have they flown,
Succeeding--still succeeding! Here the Child
Puts, when the high-swoln Flood runs fierce and wild,
His budding courage to the proof; and here
Declining Manhood learns to note the sly
And sure encroachments of infirmity,
Thinking how fast time runs, life's end how near!

X. THE SAME SUBJECT

Not so that Pair whose youthful spirits dance
With prompt emotion, urging them to pass;
A sweet confusion checks the Shepherd-lass;
Blushing she eyes the dizzy flood askance;
To stop ashamed--too timid to advance;
She ventures once again--another pause!
His outstretched hand He tauntingly withdraws--
She sues for help with piteous utterance!
Chidden she chides again; the thrilling touch
Both feel, when he renews the wished-for aid:
Ah! if their fluttering hearts should stir too much,
Should beat too strongly, both may be betrayed.
The frolic Loves, who, from yon high rock, see
The struggle, clap their wings for victory!

XI. THE FAERY CHASM

No fiction was it of the antique age:
A sky-blue stone, within this sunless cleft,
Is of the very footmarks unbereft
Which tiny Elves impressed;--on that smooth stage
Dancing with all their brilliant equipage

In secret revels--haply after theft
Of some sweet Babe--Flower stolen, and coarse Weed left
For the distracted Mother to assuage
Her grief with, as she might!--But, where, oh! where
Is traceable a vestige of the notes
That ruled those dances wild in character?--
Deep underground? Or in the upper air,
On the shrill wind of midnight? or where floats
O'er twilight fields the autumnal gossamer?

XII. HINTS FOR THE FANCY

On,, loitering Muse--the swift Stream chides us--on!
Albeit his deep-worn channel doth immure
Objects immense portrayed in miniature,
Wild shapes for many a strange comparison!
Niagaras, Alpine passes, and anon
Abodes of Naiads, calm abysses pure,
Bright liquid mansions, fashioned to endure
When the broad oak drops, a leafless skeleton,
And the solidities of mortal pride,
Palace and tower, are crumbled into dust!--
The Bard who walks with Duddon for his guide,
Shall find such toys of fancy thickly set:
Turn from the sight, enamoured Muse--we must;
And, if thou canst, leave them without regret!

XIII. OPEN PROSPECT

Hail to the fields--with Dwellings sprinkled o'er,
And one small hamlet, under a green hill
Clustering, with barn and byre, and spouting mill!
A glance suffices,--should we wish for more,
Gay June would scorn us. But when bleak winds roar
Through the stiff lance-like shoots of pollard ash,
Dread swell of sound! loud as the gusts that lash
The matted forests of Ontario's shore
By wasteful steel unsmitten--then would I
Turn into port; and, reckless of the gale,
Reckless of angry Duddon sweeping by,
While the warm hearth exalts the mantling ale,
Laugh with the generous household heartily
At all the merry pranks of Donnerdale!

XIV

O Mountain Stream! the Shepherd and his Cot
Are privileged Inmates of deep solitude;
Nor would the nicest Anchorite exclude
A field or two of brighter green, or plot
Of tillage-ground, that seemeth like a spot
Of stationary sunshine:--thou hast viewed
These only, Duddon! with their paths renewed
By fits and starts, yet this contents thee not.
Thee hath some awful Spirit impelled to leave,
Utterly to desert, the haunts of men,
Though simple thy companions were and few;
And through this wilderness a passage cleave
Attended but by thy own voice, save when
The clouds and fowls of the air thy way pursue!

1806.

XV

From this deep chasm, where quivering sunbeams play
Upon its loftiest crags, mine eyes behold
A gloomy NICHE, capacious, blank, and cold;
A concave free from shrubs and mosses grey;
In semblance fresh, as if, with dire affray,
Some Statue, placed amid these regions old
For tutelary service, thence had rolled,
Startling the flight of timid Yesterday!
Was it by mortals sculptured?--weary slaves
Of slow endeavour! or abruptly cast
Into rude shape by fire, with roaring blast
Tempestuously let loose from central caves?
Or fashioned by the turbulence of waves,
Then, when o'er highest hills the Deluge passed?

XVI. AMERICAN TRADITION

Such fruitless questions may not long beguile
Or plague the fancy 'mid the sculptured shows
Conspicuous yet where Oroonoko flows;
'There' would the Indian answer with a smile
Aimed at the White Man's ignorance, the while,
Of the GREAT WATERS telling how they rose,
Covered the plains, and, wandering where they chose,

Mounted through every intricate defile,
Triumphant--Inundation wide and deep,
O'er which his Fathers urged, to ridge and steep
Else unapproachable, their buoyant way;
And carved, on mural cliff's undreaded side,
Sun, moon, and stars, and beast of chase or prey;
Whate'er they sought, shunned, loved, or deified!

XVII. RETURN

A dark plume fetch me from yon blasted yew,
Perched on whose top the Danish Raven croaks;
Aloft, the imperial Bird of Rome invokes
Departed ages, shedding where he flew
Loose fragments of wild wailing, that bestrew
The clouds and thrill the chambers of the rocks;
And into silence hush the timorous flocks,
That, calmly couching while the nightly dew
Moistened each fleece, beneath the twinkling stars
Slept amid that lone Camp on Hardknot's height,
Whose Guardians bent the knee to Jove and Mars:
Or, near that mystic Round of Druid frame
Tardily sinking by its proper weight
Deep into patient Earth, from whose smooth breast it came!

XVIII. SEATHWAITE CHAPEL

Sacred Religion! "mother of form and fear,"
Dread arbitress of mutable respect,
New rites ordaining when the old are wrecked,
Or cease to please the fickle worshipper;
Mother of Love! (that name best suits thee here)
Mother of Love! for this deep vale, protect
Truth's holy lamp, pure source of bright effect,
Gifted to purge the vapoury atmosphere
That seeks to stifle it;--as in those days
When this low Pile a Gospel Teacher knew,
Whose good works formed an endless retinue:
A Pastor such as Chaucer's verse portrays;
Such as the heaven-taught skill of Herbert drew;
And tender Goldsmith crowned with deathless praise!

XIX. TRIBUTARY STREAM

My frame hath often trembled with delight

When hope presented some far-distant good,
That seemed from heaven descending, like the flood
Of yon pure waters, from their aery height
Hurrying, with lordly Duddon to unite;
Who, 'mid a world of images imprest
On the calm depth of his transparent breast,
Appears to cherish most that Torrent white,
The fairest, softest, liveliest of them all!
And seldom hath ear listened to a tune
More lulling than the busy hum of Noon,
Swoln by that voice--whose murmur musical
Announces to the thirsty fields a boon
Dewy and fresh, till showers again shall fall.

XX. THE PLAIN OF DONNERDALE

The old inventive Poets, had they seen,
Or rather felt, the entrancement that detains
Thy waters, Duddon! 'mid these flowery plains--
The still repose, the liquid lapse serene,
Transferred to bowers imperishably green,
Had beautified Elysium! But these chains
Will soon be broken;--a rough course remains,
Rough as the past; where Thou, of placid mien,
Innocuous as a firstling of the flock,
And countenanced like a soft cerulean sky,
Shalt change thy temper; and, with many a shock
Given and received in mutual jeopardy,
Dance, like a Bacchanal, from rock to rock,
Tossing her frantic thyrsus wide and high!

XXI

Whence that low voice?--A whisper from the heart,
That told of days long past, when here I roved
With friends and kindred tenderly beloved;
Some who had early mandates to depart,
Yet are allowed to steal my path athwart
By Duddon's side; once more do we unite,
Once more, beneath the kind Earth's tranquil light;
And smothered joys into new being start.
From her unworthy seat, the cloudy stall
Of Time, breaks forth triumphant Memory;
Her glistening tresses bound, yet light and free
As golden locks of birch, that rise and fall
On gales that breathe too gently to recall

Aught of the fading year's inclemency!

XXII. TRADITION

A love-lord Maid, at some far-distant time,
Came to this hidden pool, whose depths surpass
In crystal clearness Dian's looking-glass;
And, gazing, saw that Rose, which from the prime
Derives its name, reflected, as the chime
Of echo doth reverberate some sweet sound:
The starry treasure from the blue profound
She longed to ravish;--shall she plunge, or climb
The humid precipice, and seize the guest
Of April, smiling high in upper air?
Desperate alternative! what fiend could dare
To prompt the thought?--Upon the steep rock's breast
The lonely Primrose yet renews its bloom,
Untouched memento of her hapless doom!

XXIII. SHEEP-WASHING

Sad thoughts, avaunt!--partake we their blithe cheer
Who gathered in betimes the unshorn flock
To wash the fleece, where haply bands of rock,
Checking the stream, make a pool smooth and clear
As this we look on. Distant Mountains hear,
Hear and repeat, the turmoil that unites
Clamour of boys with innocent despites
Of barking dogs, and bleatings from strange fear.
And what if Duddon's spotless flood receive
Unwelcome mixtures as the uncouth noise
Thickens, the pastoral River will forgive
Such wrong; nor need 'we' blame the licensed joys,
Though false to Nature's quiet equipoise:
Frank are the sports, the stains are fugitive.

XXIV. THE RESTING-PLACE

Mid-noon is past;--upon the sultry mead
No zephyr breathes, no cloud its shadow throws:
If we advance unstrengthened by repose,
Farewell the solace of the vagrant reed!
This Nook--with woodbine hung and straggling weed
Tempting recess as ever pilgrim chose,
Half grot, half arbour--proffers to enclose

Body and mind, from molestation freed,
In narrow compass--narrow as itself:
Or if the Fancy, too industrious Elf,
Be loth that we should breathe awhile exempt
From new incitements friendly to our task,
Here wants not stealthy prospect, that may tempt
Loose Idless to forego her wily mask.

XXV

Methinks 'twere no unprecedented feat
Should some benignant Minister of air
Lift, and encircle with a cloudy chair,
The One for whom my heart shall ever beat
With tenderest love;--or, if a safer seat
Atween his downy wings be furnished, there
Would lodge her, and the cherished burden bear
O'er hill and valley to this dim retreat!
Rough ways my steps have trod;--too rough and long
For her companionship; here dwells soft ease:
With sweets that she partakes not some distaste
Mingles, and lurking consciousness of wrong;
Languish the flowers; the waters seem to waste
Their vocal charm; their sparklings cease to please.

XXVI

Return, Content! for fondly I pursued,
Even when a child, the Streams--unheard, unseen;
Through tangled woods, impending rocks between;
Or, free as air, with flying inquest viewed
The sullen reservoirs whence their bold brood--
Pure as the morning, fretful, boisterous, keen,
Green as the salt-sea billows, white and green--
Poured down the hills, a choral multitude!
Nor have I tracked their course for scanty gains;
They taught me random cares and truant joys,
That shield from mischief and preserve from stains
Vague minds, while men are growing out of boys;
Maturer Fancy owes to their rough noise
Impetuous thoughts that brook not servile reins.

XXVII

Fallen, and diffused into a shapeless heap,

Or quietly self-buried in earth's mould,
Is that embattled House, whose massy Keep,
Flung from yon cliff a shadow large and cold.
There dwelt the gay, the bountiful, the bold;
Till nightly lamentations, like the sweep
Of winds--though winds were silent--struck a deep
And lasting terror through that ancient Hold.
Its line of Warriors fled;--they shrunk when tried
By ghostly power:--but Time's unsparing hand
Hath plucked such foes, like weeds, from out the land;
And now, if men with men in peace abide,
All other strength the weakest may withstand,
All worse assaults may safely be defied.

XXVIII. JOURNEY RENEWED

I rose while yet the cattle, heat-opprest,
Crowded together under rustling trees
Brushed by the current of the water-breeze;
And for 'their' sakes, and love of all that rest,
On Duddon's margin, in the sheltering nest;
For all the startled scaly tribes that slink
Into his coverts, and each fearless link
Of dancing insects forged upon his breast;
For these, and hopes and recollections worn
Close to the vital seat of human clay;
Glad meetings, tender partings, that upstay
The drooping mind of absence, by vows sworn
In his pure presence near the trysting thorn--
I thanked the Leader of my onward way.

XXIX

No record tells of lance opposed to lance,
Horse charging horse, 'mid these retired domains;
Tells that their turf drank purple from the veins
Of heroes, fallen, or struggling to advance,
Till doubtful combat issued in a trance
Of victory, that struck through heart and reins
Even to the inmost seat of mortal pains,
And lightened o'er the pallid countenance.
Yet, to the loyal and the brave, who lie
In the blank earth, neglected and forlorn,
The passing Winds memorial tribute pay;
The Torrents chant their praise, inspiring scorn
Of power usurped; with proclamation high,

And glad acknowledgment, of lawful sway.

XXX

Who swerves from innocence, who makes divorce
Of that serene companion--a good name,
Recovers not his loss; but walks with shame,
With doubt, with fear, and haply with remorse:
And oft-times he--who, yielding to the force
Of chance-temptation, ere his journey end,
From chosen comrade turns, or faithful friend--
In vain shall rue the broken intercourse.
Not so with such as loosely wear the chain
That binds them, pleasant River! to thy side:--
Through the rough copse wheel thou with hasty stride;
I choose to saunter o'er the grassy plain,
Sure, when the separation has been tried,
That we, who part in love, shall meet again.

XXXI

The kirk of Ulpha to the pilgrim's eye
Is welcome as a star, that doth present
Its shining forehead through the peaceful rent
Of a black cloud diffused o'er half the sky:
Or as a fruitful palm-tree towering high
O'er the parched waste beside an Arab's tent;
Or the Indian tree whose branches, downward bent,
Take root again, a boundless canopy.
How sweet were leisure! could it yield no more
Than 'mid that wave-washed Churchyard to recline,
From pastoral graves extracting thoughts divine;
Or there to pace, and mark the summits hoar
Of distant moonlit mountains faintly shine,
Soothed by the unseen River's gentle roar.

XXXII

Not hurled precipitous from steep to steep;
Lingering no more 'mid flower-enamelled lands
And blooming thickets; nor by rocky bands
Held; but in radiant progress toward the Deep
Where mightiest rivers into powerless sleep
Sink, and forget heir nature--'now' expands
Majestic Duddon, over smooth flat sands

Gliding in silence with unfettered sweep!
Beneath an ampler sky a region wide
Is opened round him:--hamlets, towers, and towns,
And blue-topped hills, behold him from afar;
In stately mien to sovereign Thames allied
Spreading his bosom under Kentish downs,
With commerce freighted, or triumphant war.

XXXIII. CONCLUSION

Buthere no cannon thunders to the gale;
Upon the wave no haughty pendants cast
A crimson splendour: lowly is the mast
That rises here, and humbly spread, the sail;
While, less disturbed than in the narrow Vale
Through which with strange vicissitudes he passed,
The Wanderer seeks that receptacle vast
Where all his unambitious functions fail
And may thy Poet, cloud-born Stream! be free--
The sweets of earth contentedly resigned,
And each tumultuous working left behind
At seemly distance--to advance like Thee;
Prepared, in peace of heart, in calm of mind
And soul, to mingle with Eternity!

XXXIV. AFTER-THOUGHT

I thought of Thee, my partner and my guide,
As being past away.--Vain sympathies!
For, backward, Duddon, as I cast my eyes,
I see what was, and is, and will abide;
Still glides the Stream, and shall for ever glide;
The Form remains, the Function never dies;
While we, the brave, the mighty, and the wise,
We Men, who in our morn of youth defied
The elements, must vanish;--be it so!
Enough, if something from our hands have power
To live, and act, and serve the future hour;
And if, as toward the silent tomb we go,
Through love, through hope, and faith's transcendent dower,
We feel that we are greater than we know.

William Wordsworth – A Short Biography

William Wordsworth was born on 7 April, 1770 in Cockermouth, in Cumbria, northwest England.

A poet of world class stature and authority his initial introduction to poetry came from his father, John Wordsworth. But his frequent absences meant that William was essentially raised by his Mother's parents in Penrith and these times were endured by William as a painful period of conflict and dark thoughts of suicide.

But the landscape surrounding him did eventually seep into him and he would walk for many hours in the fells of the Lake District often with his sister, Dorothy, to whom he was increasingly attached.

In 1778, the young William was sent to Hawkshead Grammar School in Lancashire; he was to now be separated from Dorothy for nine years. At Hawkshead he received an excellent education encompassing classics, literature, and mathematics, but for him there was the greater education to indulge in; the boyhood pleasures of living and playing in the outdoors. The natural scenery of the English lakes could terrify as well as nurture, as Wordsworth would write "I grew up fostered alike by beauty and by fear,"

By 1787, he had arrived at St. John's College, Cambridge and also to publish his first poem, a sonnet for the European magazine. But he distanced himself from the competitive pressures of University life and idled his way through saying he "was not for that hour, nor for that place."

In 1790, whilst still at Cambridge he travelled to France. He was immediately taken by the Revolutionary fervor and the confluence of a set of great ideals and rallying calls for the people of France.

Upon taking his Cambridge degree, an un-ambitious "pass", he returned in 1791 to France, where he met and began an affair with Annette Vallon. Their illegitimate child, Anne Caroline, was born in December 1792. Wordsworth wanted to marry but returned alone to England. The beginning of hostilities between England and France meant he would not see his daughter until she was nine but he maintained his financial obligations to his daughter whilst keeping her hidden from the public gaze.

For Wordsworth this blow was compounded by the 'Reign of Terror' and its trampling upon the ideals of 'liberté, égalité, fraternité'.

There now followed a period of three to four years that plagued Wordsworth with doubt. He was now in his early thirties but had no profession, was rootless and virtually penniless as well as being totally opposed to his country's position on the French. He lived in London with radicals such as William Godwin and felt profound sympathy for the abandoned mothers, beggars, children, vagrants, and victims of England's wars who began to take form in the darker, more melancholy poems he began writing at this time.

Although his career was not on track he did manage to publish two volumes, both in 1793; An Evening Walk and Descriptive Sketches.

This dark period ended in 1795. A legacy of £900 received from Raisley Calvert enabled Wordsworth to pursue a literary career in earnest.

This bequest almost made possible a reunion with his beloved sister Dorothy. They were never to be apart again and they moved in 1797 to Alfoxden House, near Bristol.

It was here that Wordsworth now became great friends with a fellow poet, Samuel Taylor Coleridge. They formed a partnership that would change both their lives and the course of English poetry.

This next year when Wordsworth and Coleridge were "together wantoned in wild Poesy," had two direct results for Wordsworth. Firstly he moved away from the long poems he had been laboring upon; these included poems of social protest like Salisbury Plain, loco-descriptive poems such as An Evening Walk and Descriptive Sketches, and The Borderers, a blank-verse tragedy exploring the psychology of guilt (published only in 1842).

Emboldened by Coleridge and under the marveling influences of nature and his sister, Wordsworth began to write the short lyrical and dramatic poems for which he is best remembered.

The aim of much of these short works was to provide a decisive break with the strictures of Neoclassical verse. They first appeared in 1798 in a slim, anonymously authored volume entitled Lyrical Ballads. Wordsworth wrote in the preface "the spontaneous overflow of powerful feelings: it takes its origin from emotion recollected in tranquility." The book began with Coleridge's long poem "The Rime of the Ancient Mariner" and ended with Wordsworth's "Tintern Abbey."

All but three of the other poems were written by Wordsworth. Two years later in a preface to a second edition he wrote that their objective was "to choose incidents and situations from common life and to relate or describe them...in a selection of language really used by men...tracing in them...the primary laws of our nature."

Most of the poems were dramatic in form, designed to reveal the character of the speaker. Thus the poems set forth a new style, a new vocabulary, and new subjects for poetry.

The second consequence of Wordsworth's work with Coleridge was the structuring of a vastly ambitious poetic design that teased and haunted him for the rest of his life.

Coleridge had conceived of an enormous poem to be called "The Brook," in which he proposed to treat all science, philosophy, and religion, but he soon laid the burden of writing this poem upon Wordsworth himself.

As early as 1798 Wordsworth began to talk in grand terms of this poem, to be entitled The Recluse. To nerve himself up to this enterprise and to test his powers, Wordsworth began writing the autobiographical poem that would absorb him intermittently for the next 40 years, and which was eventually published in 1850 under the title The Prelude, or, Growth of a Poet's Mind.

The Recluse itself was never completed; only one of its three parts was actually written; this was published in 1814 as The Excursion and consisted of nine long philosophical monologues spoken by pastoral characters.

Wordsworth and Dorothy spent the winter of 1798–99 in Germany, where, in Goslar, in Saxony, he experienced the most intense isolation he had ever known. But the result was some of his most moving poetry, including the "Lucy" and "Matthew" elegies and early drafts toward The Prelude.

Upon his return to England, Wordsworth incorporated several of these into the second edition of Lyrical Ballads. Together with the astounding work of his second verse collection, Poems, in Two Volumes (1807), it is often said that the period from 1797-1808 was Wordsworth's great decade.

In 1802, during the Peace of Amiens, Wordsworth returned to France, and in Calais he met his daughter, Anne Caroline, and made his peace with her mother, Annette.

That done he journeyed once more back to England and to marriage with Mary Hutchinson, a childhood friend, and to start another family of three sons and two daughters, although only two children would survive.

In 1805 the drowning of Wordsworth's favorite brother, John, the captain of a sailing vessel, gave Wordsworth the strongest shock he had ever experienced. "A deep distress hath humanized my Soul,"

In 1813, he received an appointment as Distributor of Stamps for Westmorland which had an annual income of £400 gave him the financial security to devote his spare time to poetry and to move his family into Rydal Mount, Grasmere; a beautiful location, which inspired his later poetry.

By the 1820s, the critical acclaim for Wordsworth was growing, though his poetry was losing its earlier vigor and emotional luster. For many years Wordsworth had been assailed by vicious, tireless attacks by the critics. Only with the publication of The River Duddon in 1820, did the tide begin to turn.

Many of Wordsworth's last years were given over to tinkering and revising his poems rather than embark on new works.

His masterpiece, The Prelude, had four distinct manuscript versions (1798–99, 1805–06, 1818–20, and 1832–39) and was published only after the poet's death in 1850.

In 1839 he received an honorary degree from Oxford University and received a civil pension of £300 a year from the government.

With the death in 1843 of his friend and Poet Laureate Robert Southey, Wordsworth was offered the position. He accepted despite saying he wouldn't write any poetry as Poet Laureate. Indeed it is still unfortunate that Wordsworth is still the only Poet Laureate never to write any poems during his time as Poet Laureate.

Wordsworth died of pleurisy on 23 April 1850. He was buried in St Oswald's church Grasmere.

As a poet his work is still avidly read today. He is acknowledged as one of the Romantic Poets, A Lake Poet and a writer of immense talent who gave a voice to many and varied thoughts.

William Wordsworth – A Concise Bibliography

Major Works
Descriptive Sketches (1793)
An Evening Walk (1793)
Lyrical Ballads, with a Few Other Poems (1798)

"Simon Lee"
"We are Seven"
"Lines Written in Early Spring"
"Expostulation and Reply"
"The Tables Turned"
"The Thorn"
"Lines Composed A Few Miles Above Tintern Abbey"
Lyrical Ballads, with Other Poems (1800)
Preface to the Lyrical Ballads
"Strange Fits of Passion Have I Known"
"She Dwelt Among the Untrodden Ways"
"Three Years She Grew"
"A Slumber Did my Spirit Seal"
"I Travelled Among Unknown Men"
"Lucy Gray"
"The Two April Mornings"
"Nutting"
"The Ruined Cottage"
"Michael"
"The Kitten At Play"
Poems, in Two Volumes (1807)
"Resolution and Independence"
"I Wandered Lonely as a Cloud" (aka "Daffodils")
"My Heart Leaps Up"
"Ode: Intimations of Immortality"
"Ode to Duty"
"The Solitary Reaper"
"Elegiac Stanzas"
"Composed Upon Westminster Bridge, September 3, 1802"
"London, 1802"
"The World Is Too Much with Us"
Guide to the Lakes (1810)
"To the Cuckoo"
The Excursion (1814)
Laodamia (1815, 1845)
The Borderers (1842)
The Prelude (1850)